THE LIFE & TIMES OF

Anne Frank

BY
Rosanna Kelly

‖ •PARRAGON• ‖

This edition first published by Parragon Books

Produced by
Magpie Books Ltd
7 Kensington Church Court
London W8 4SP

Illustrations courtesy of: ANNE FRANK–Fonds, Basel,
Switzerland; Mary Evans Picture Library; Rex Features;
Associated Press.

ISBN 1 85813 957 0

A copy of the British Library Cataloguing in Publication
Data is available from the British Library.

Typeset by Hewer Text Composition Services, Edinburgh
Printed in Singapore by Printlink International Co.

A CAREFREE CHILDHOOD

Anne Frank was born on 12 June 1929 in the German city of Frankfurt am Main. It was also the birthplace of her father, Otto Heinrich Frank (born on 12 May 1889), the son of a successful business man, Michael Frank, and a rich local heiress, Alice Betty Stern, who could trace her ancestors back to the seventeenth century in the city archives.

The Franks belonged to the liberal Jewish middle classes. As Reform Jews, they observed the traditions of the Jewish religion without adhering strictly to all Jewish beliefs and customs. Frankfurt, at that time, had the second largest Jewish community in Germany after Berlin. Since the beginning of the nineteenth century, Jews had been allowed to live outside the ghetto and the law declared them equal citizens.

Anne's father grew up in a large house, with parties every week, balls, festivities, waltzing and dinners. After attending the Lessing Secondary School in Frankfurt, he studied art at the University of Heidelberg, but abandoned his studies when the opportunity arose for him to go and work in New York. There he stayed for a year until news of his father's death in the autumn of 1909 brought him back to Germany. He was to continue his business training in

Dusseldorf until the outbreak of the First World War.

After joining the German army in 1915, he was assigned to an artillery regiment and sent to the Western Front. He was quickly promoted to the rank of lieutenant. The end of the war saw him back in Frankfurt, where he settled down as an independent business man, specializing in banking.

The high inflation of 1922–23 had a disastrous effect on the Frank family fortune and on Germany in general, humiliated by defeat and facing an economic crisis. Workers were losing their jobs; farmers their land; civilians their savings. In such testing conditions, it was all Mr Frank could do to keep his father's bank afloat. In fact, all the firm's activities were to cease in 1934.

Mr Frank wore a moustache and was tall and slim. Modest and kind, he was an intelligent and cultured man. In the spring of 1925, aged thirty-six, he married Edith Hollander, the daughter of a wealthy manufacturer from Aachen, a German town close to the Dutch border. She was then twenty-five. The marriage took place in a synagogue in Aachen on 12 May. Their first daughter, Margot Betti, was born in 1926, followed by Anneliese Mary, called Anne, in 1929.

1929 was the start of the Great Depression. Life in Germany had become very hard. Poverty and unemployment were at an all-time high, not least in Frankfurt, where more than 70,000 people would be without a job by 1932. Many Germans felt disillusioned with their government, and turned instead to the German National Socialist Labour Party, more often known as the Nazi Party, an organisation founded by Adolf Hitler in 1919. Hitler preached that the Germans were a superior race, and won support by blaming the Jews for all the problems in Germany. Such was the world into which Anne was born.

Anne's first year was spent at 307 Marbach-weg, a house with green shutters and a birch in the front garden, where Mr and Mrs Frank and Margot had been living since 1927. The family would stay there for a little more than a year, moving to 24 Ganghoferstrasse in another part of Frankfurt in March 1931. There were lovely walks in the neighbour-hood, and hills where they could go tobog-ganing in the winter.

From the first, Anne was the exact opposite

of Margot, although she clearly looked up to her older sister. Margot was a very pretty, quiet and sensible girl. Anne was the naughty little sister, and was constantly getting into trouble. However, she was to develop great charm and a good sense of humour.

Four years passed. At the end of January 1933 the Franks were visiting friends when they heard the news that Hitler had become Chancellor of Germany. The reaction of their host was cheerful, but Mr Frank was speechless, and his wife sat as if she had been turned to stone. Both realised that life in Germany would now become intolerable for them.

Within two months the Nazi Party had won the municipal elections in Frankfurt. The next day, the liberal Jewish mayor was forced to resign, and it was not long before all Jewish employees of the city had been dismissed. In the mean time, on 23 March 1933, Hitler had seized control. Mr Frank foresaw that Hitler's rise to power boded extreme hardship for the Jewish people. Some 300,000 Jews, about half the Jewish population, would leave Germany between 1933 and 1939. In the summer of 1933 Mr Frank took his wife and two daughters to stay with Edith's mother in Aachen. He went on to Amsterdam. He was to set up new business there, and had the task of finding another home for his family.

The new company that Mr Frank set up in Amsterdam was a subsidiary of a larger firm in Germany. Known as Opekta-works, the firm manufactured and traded in pectin, a powdered fruit extract used to make jam and jellies. The little jam-making kits were sold to Dutch housewives. One of the first people to be employed by the company was Miep Santroushitz, a young Austrian woman who had lived in Holland for some time. Another important member of the office staff was a man called Victor Kugler. Aged about thirty-three, he was good-looking, dark-haired and precise. Mr Frank was able to register the new business with the Amsterdam Chamber of Commerce and Industry in September 1933.

Next, Mr Frank found a suitable apartment for his family. In December, Edith and Margot came to join him from Germany, followed by Anne in March of the new year. Edith's mother was to come later, when the situation in Germany had become so intolerable that she was forced to leave her home, aged seventy-three. Holland, at that time, was home to many refugees. Some 24,000 Jewish people fled there for safety after Hitler came to power. Amsterdam had the largest Jewish population, numbering about 9,000.

The Franks quickly settled down in their new home in South Amsterdam. It was an apartment in a modern block of flats on the Merwedeplein, a large square with an immense lawn in the middle of it. Mr and Mrs Frank enrolled their daughters at a nearby Montessori school, where they learned Dutch, and soon made new friends, including the children of several other Jewish families who had escaped from Germany.

It was a happy time for Anne. She loved her school, and her home life on the Merwedeplein. One of her favourite games was hopscotch on the pavement outside the flat, but she also joined in with the other children at turning cart-wheels and practising hand-stands. Her one regret was that she could not whistle like the rest of her friends, but she made up for this defect by singing instead.

By the time she was ten years old, Anne had become quite a personality. She liked acting in school plays, and was always chattering about her many schoolfriends and her visits to their homes. She was enthusiastic about many things, from the latest films to history and mythology. Rather thin and delicate, she had deeply set dark eyes, shiny dark hair, and dimples in her cheeks when she smiled. Margot was also growing up and becoming even prettier. An intelligent girl, she did extremely well at school.

By 1939 Mr Frank's firm had diversified and expanded, as had his staff. Besides Miep and Mr Kugler, there were three new people. The first, Mr Van Pels, was an old acquaintance of Mr Frank's and, like him, a refugee from Germany. He had come in as an adviser on the spice business. The second, Bep Voskuijl, was the office girl. Young and very shy, with brownish-blonde hair and glasses, she was quickly taken under Miep's kindly wing. The third was Mr Kleiman, a quiet, kind, frail-looking man, with large, thick glasses. The future of Mr Frank's firm would have been bright, had it not been for the outbreak of World War 11 in 1939, and Hitler's invasion of Holland on 10 May 1940. From 15 May, the country was under German occupation.

Edith Frank with Margot and Anne in Frankfurt

Hitler's troops invaded Holland on 10 May 1940

INTO HIDING

After the occupation, a strange air of uncertainty settled over Holland as the Dutch waited to see what would happen next. At first, life continued as usual. However, as winter approached, the Nazis introduced many measures that were calculated to make the situation of Dutch Jews increasingly uncomfortable. In November 1940, all Jewish civil servants were dismissed. Then signs started appearing on park benches and in public places, saying 'Not for Jews' or 'Jews not wanted here'. Next, the Nazis issued a decree, calling for notification of all enterprises which were owned or directed by Jews. It was the first step towards the complete 'dejudification' of Dutch businesses. Mr Frank, who had followed similar developments in Germany, took the precaution of transferring the ownership of his business to his two non-Jewish Dutch associates, Mr Kugler and Mr Kleiman. The business was now renamed Trading Company Gies & Co, after Miep's husband Jan Gies.

In the course of the next year, it became impossible for Jewish people to live a normal life. The anti-Jewish decrees exluded Jews from cinemas and public parks, and prohibited them from travelling by tram. After the summer holidays in 1941, schools were racially segregated. Anne and Margot, and eighty-five other Jewish children from their Montessori school,   had to transfer to a Jewish school with only Jewish teachers. It was not long before Otto, Edith, Margot and Anne Frank were forced to wear the yellow star which became obligatory for all Jews from May 1942.

Fearing that greater persecution was coming to Holland, Mr Frank made an attempt to emigrate with his family in January 1942. In the mean time, in case his application was unsuccessful, he was secretly preparing to go into hiding. The hiding-place was to be behind the two upper back floors of his company offices, now run by Mr Kleiman and Mr Kugler, at Prinsengracht 263. It was an old, narrow building on the bank of a canal,   in a street lined with other small factories and warehouses. The escape was only made possible by the courage and loyal friendship of Mr Kugler, Mr Kleiman, Miep and Bep. They all promised to keep the secret and help the family while they were in hiding. Mr Frank also arranged for his business partner, Mr Van Pels, to join them with his family.

On the first Sunday of July 1942, Margot Frank was one of a thousand Jews to receive a notice with an order to report for work at a German labour camp (the Nazi euphemism for a concentration camp). It was the latest of a series of call-ups that the Nazis had introduced in January 1942. They had started by taking unemployed Jewish men; then entire families were summoned; and now it was Margot. Faced with the choice of either obeying the Gestapo or going 'underground', the Franks decided to go into hiding immediately. Hearing what had happened, Miep and her husband Jan Gies came round to the panic-stricken flat on the Merwedeplein to help the family pack. Miep recalled how Anne came into the room bringing too many things, and was told by her mother to take them back. Her eyes were like saucers, a mixture of excitement and terrible fright. Among the things that Anne put into her own satchel were the diary which she had been given by her parents for her thirteenth birthday several weeks earlier, her curlers, a handkerchief, some schoolbooks, a comb and a few letters. As she wrote in her diary: 'Memories mean more to me than dresses.'

Early the next day, Miep came back to the flat on her bicycle to fetch Margot. It was pouring with rain. Margot filled her satchel with schoolbooks, fetched her bicycle and

rode after Miep through the downpour.
Meanwhile, at half-past seven, Anne and
her parents closed the door of their flat,
leaving everything they owned behind
them. Anne's only farewell was to
Moortje, her little cat. The Franks left some
meat for him in the kitchen, and a note to
the neighbours asking them to look after
him. As Anne and her parents walked
through the rain, each with a school satchel
and shopping-bag filled to the brim, Anne
noticed the sympathetic looks they were
being given by people on their way to
work. Their faces told how sorry they were
that they could not offer them a lift, but the
yellow star spoke for itself.

The distance between the flat and Mr Frank's
offices on Prinsengracht was about two and a
half miles. Miep was there to greet them

when they arrived. Later, she recalled that all three were quite wet, were carrying a few things and had yellow stars sewn on to their clothes. She quickly took them upstairs to the back of the office and into the secret wing, where Margot was waiting for her family. Then Miep left them all to settle in their new rooms and recover.

Anne was surrounded by a jumble of sacks and boxes and furnishings, brought secretly during the previous months. While Mrs Frank and Margot, looking white and exhausted, sank down into their unmade beds, Anne and her father set about the task of creating some order out of the chaos. By the evening they were tired out, having unpacked boxes, filled cupboards, and hammered and tidied all day.

The four small rooms and attic belonged to a house, not visible from the street, behind the main offices of Trading Company Gies & Co. From the front warehouse, Miep had led them upstairs to a landing and through a little grey door which had opened to reveal the Secret Annexe. For greater safety this door would be camouflaged behind a movable bookcase a month after the Franks moved in.

Immediately inside the Secret Annexe was a steep staircase, to the right of which was a tiny windowless room containing a washbasin and a WC. On the left of the steps, a passage gave access to two other small rooms, each with a window looking on to a courtyard behind. The first was to be the bedsitting-room of Mr and Mrs Frank; the second, long and narrow, belonged to Margot and Anne. Up the steep flight of old

Anne at her desk in 1941
Copyright ANNE FRANK – Fonds, Basel

Anne and Otto on their way to Miep's wedding

wooden steps was a much larger space, with sink, stove and cabinets. Previously used as a laboratory, it would serve as the kitchen, and also as Mr and Mrs Van Pels' bedroom. Another rickety staircase led from this floor to an attic storage area, cutting through a tiny garret, where Peter, the Van Pels' fifteen-year-old son, would sleep.

The house was damp and leaned to one side, but it would have been hard to discover a better hiding-place anywhere in Amsterdam. Moreover, it was unusual to find a place where a whole family could hide. In the Netherlands, most of the families of the 25,000 Jewish people in hiding were separated. Many children, sent to hide with farmers in the countryside, never saw their parents again. Of all those who went 'underground', some 16,000 survived the war.

The remaining 9,000 people were discovered and deported. Often they had been betrayed.

LIFE IN THE SECRET ANNEXE

On the morning of 13 July, at around breakfast time, the Van Pels family arrived in the Secret Annexe. To the great amusement of Anne, Mrs Van Pels came with a large chamber-pot in her hat-box. Mr Van Pels, her father's jocular partner at the office, was a large man, with a cigarette always dangling from his mouth. Peter, their son, was a shy, gawky youth, but Anne immediately took to his cat, Mouschi, although she still missed her

own kitten, Moortje. The family had brought
forward the date of their disappearance because there had been a spate of *razzias*, the
Nazi round-ups of Jewish people for deporta-
tion. An account of the extra week they had
spent in the outside world was eagerly sought
by the Franks, who were reassured and
amused to learn that all their neighbours
believed they had fled to Switzerland.

The Van Pels family were soon installed in
the Annexe. For the first few weeks, everyone lived in constant terror of being discovered, taking endless care, while people were
working in the office below, not to be seen
or heard. Margot was forbidden to cough at
night, even though she had a bad cold. It
must have been maddening for the energetic
Anne to have to sit still for hours – but she
had to and she did. The only amusements

were reading, studying and the radio. Apart from that, everyone looked forward to the daily visits of their helpers, who brought them food and books, and kept them informed of what was happening in Amsterdam.

In the months to come, Anne's best friend was to be the diary that her parents had given her. Her letters to 'Kitty', an imaginary friend she confided in completely, helped her to unburden herself of feelings and thoughts which it was impossible to tell anyone else about. She tried to analyse her own nature, and record her impressions of living in close confinement with the others.

As the youngest of the group, Anne became the target for the sermonizing of the four adults, but she learned not to answer back and to keep her thoughts to herself. Her wish was to improve herself, and she knew her own faults and shortcomings better than anyone else. As time went by, Anne also changed her opinion of the six people she was with. She noted in her diary on 21 August 1942 that she and Mr Van Pels usually managed to upset each other, but that he seemed to like Margot very much; yet later she saw a great improvement in their relationship. The only person she consistently looked up to was her father. A soft word from him made a far greater impression on her than any shouting.

Most of the time, life in the Annexe was one of dreariness, overcast by a mood of gloom when distressing news was received from the outside world. The Franks knew, for instance, that the *razzias* were still continu-

The house at Prinsengracht 263

After the war, a Dutch journal records the persecution of the Jews

ing, and that many of their friends had been sent to concentration camps. Meanwhile, the cramped conditions began to play on the group's nerves. Relations between Edith Frank and Mrs Van Pels were far from perfect; in fact, they were often in a state of war. The critical remarks that Mrs Van Pels aimed at Margot and Anne about their poor upbringing upset Mrs Frank. The fact that the Van Pels' dinner service was in use was a constant source of irritation to Mrs Van Pels. Matters were not improved when Anne accidentally smashed one of her soup plates.

Something occurred on Tuesday, 20 October 1942, to give the seven people in hiding a terrible shock: the sound of hammering outside on the landing, at a time when nobody was making any effort to keep quiet. Someone knocked on the bookcase

door; then there was a sound of pulling and
pushing. Just as everyone thought their last
hour had come, they heard Mr Kleiman's
familiar voice. The hook which held the
door closed had jammed, and it had been
impossible to open it. The reason for his visit
was to warn them that a carpenter was
working in the house, and therefore the
rule of silence had to be obeyed. Some
time passed before the frightened inmates
of the Annexe were able to laugh about their
desperate anxiety.

Another month was gone, and with it Peter
Van Pels' sixteenth birthday on 8 November
1942. His presents included a game of
Monopoly, a razor and a lighter. It was
now announced that the Secret Annexe
was to take in an eighth person. His name
was Fritz Pfeffer. He was a dentist, and

someone the Franks had known for several years. At the appointed hour on the morning of Monday, 16 November, Miep brought Mr Pfeffer into the hiding-place and upstairs to the Van Pels' living room, where everyone was waiting for him. Not surprisingly, Mr Pfeffer looked as if he was about to faint: he believed that the Franks had fled to Belgium and then gone to Switzerland. Instead of living safely in another country, here they all were in the very centre of Amsterdam.

It had been arranged before Mr Pfeffer's arrival that Margot would move into her parents' room, and Anne would share the little room with her parents' friend. Prepared at first to like him, Anne found that within a month her view of Mr Pfeffer had changed. At the end of November, she wrote in her diary: 'It was always said about Mr Pfeffer that he could get on wonderfully with children and that he loved them all. Now he shows himself in his true colours: a stodgy, old-fashioned disciplinarian, and a preacher of long, drawn-out sermons on manners.' The place had indeed become rather cramped with eight people instead of seven.

It was now the winter of 1942. More than six months had gone by since the Franks' disappearance. St Nicholas Day was approaching, and Miep and Bep decided to make it a celebration for the three children. As a surprise, they hid a big basket, filled with little presents and poems, in a cupboard in the Annexe. It was a great success, delighting Margot, Anne and Peter. Anne wrote: 'None of us had ever celebrated St Nicholas. It was a good way of starting.'

The New Year arrived, bringing with it abysmal weather. Every night there was the rumble of hundreds of Allied planes flying over Amsterdam, heading towards bombing raids on German towns. The eight people in hiding listened to the roar of the German anti-aircraft guns shooting into the sky. On such evenings, Anne was often terrified. The door of her parents' room would creak open, and a little girl would glide into sight, clasping a pillow. She would creep into her father's bed for comfort.

There was another danger. At the end of February the owner of the office premises decided to sell the house without informing Mr Kugler or Mr Kleiman. Mr Kleiman was nearly forced to show the rooms at the back of the house to the new owner and an architect accompanying him, but claimed to have lost the key to the communicating door. Moving to another location was out of the question, since there was nowhere to go. The only hope for those in the secret wing was that the new owner would not return and ask to see anything more. He did not come back. The people in hiding also feared a burglary, as the thieves might find them and betray them to the police. On the morning of Friday, 16 July 1943, burglars did enter the warehouse, stealing two cash-boxes and coupons for 150 kilos of sugar. Fortunately, they did not discover the hidden door.

By now, Anne was fourteen years old, and growing so fast that she could no longer get into a single pair of shoes, while her vests were so small that they did not cover her stomach. One of her greatest difficulties was knowing how to get on with her mother. Mrs Frank felt hurt when her attempts to be affectionate towards her younger daughter were met with coldness. On one occasion when Anne was unfriendly, Mrs Frank left the room with tears in her eyes. Though Anne knew she was expected to apologise, she felt she could not have acted any differently.

It was now more than a year since they went into hiding, and the days had settled down into a routine. From half-past eight in the morning until half-past twelve, all was quiet. It was a time for reading and study. When the office-workers went home for lunch, the Annexe started buzzing with activity: Mrs Van Pels cleaning her only carpet with the

hoover; Margot disappearing with a few
books under her arm for her Dutch lesson;
Mr Frank finding a corner where he could
read his beloved Dickens; Mrs Frank hurry-
ing upstairs to prepare the lunch; and Anne
going to the bathroom to tidy it up, and
herself at the same time. At about a quarter to
one, the helpers arrived: Mr Kleiman or Mr
Kugler with the latest news from town, or
Bep and Miep to ask for a shopping-list. At
one o'clock everyone listened to the BBC.
Lunch was served from a quarter past one to
a quarter to two, and then everyone found
their own occupations: Margot and Mrs
Frank to the dishes; Mr and Mrs Van Pels
to their divan; Peter up to the attic; Mr Frank
downstairs; Mr Pfeffer to his bed; and Anne
to her study. Peace reigned until half-past
five, the moment when the warehousemen,
who had returned during the afternoon,

went home, and one of the helpers would come in for a chat or to bring provisions. From half-past six to seven o'clock, it was the evening meal. At nine o'clock, everyone began preparing for bed. At ten o'clock, there was the creaking of beds and a sighing of broken springs. Then all was quiet, unless Mr and Mrs Van Pels had decided to have a quarrel in bed.

The autumn of 1943 brought good news: on 8 September, Italy, a friend of Germany, surrendered to the Allies. An end to the suffering seemed in sight. Still, they had their troubles too: Mr Kleiman, who was always cheerful and brave, had to go into hospital for at least four weeks to have a stomach operation; and relations between the group were getting worse all the time. 'At mealtimes,' Anne wrote in her diary on

16 September 1943, 'no one dares to open their mouths (except to allow a mouthful of food to slip in) because whatever is said you either annoy someone or it is misunderstood.' The atmosphere in the Annexe seemed more oppressive than ever. At times Anne felt like ' a songbird whose wings have been clipped and who is hurling himself in utter darkness against the bars of his cage.'

The bookcase hiding the entrance to the Secret Annexe

The wall of Anne and Margot's room
Copyright ANNE FRANK – Fonds, Basel

A BORN WRITER

Christmas and the New Year were over, and Anne reflected that her thoughts and feelings were changing. She had acquired a new maturity. With patience and a great deal of forced cheerfulness, she was learning what her mother called 'the art of living'. She hoped, in fact, that she would no longer make her mother cry. Something was happening to her physically, too. She had become a young woman. It was difficult to discuss the changes with anybody, but she wondered at them with secret pleasure – not only at what could be seen on her body, but at all that was taking place inside her. In the mean time, she had a new craze for dancing and ballet, practising her dance-steps diligently every evening in a frock she had made out of a light blue petticoat and some ribbons.

The longing to talk to someone became so intense that Anne decided to choose Peter Van Pels. Though a slow student, and quiet, he was a simple, lovable boy, with blue-grey eyes and a mop of curly brown hair. She tried to think of an excuse to stay in his attic room and get him talking, without it being too noticeable. Her chance lay in assisting him with his crossword puzzles, and that is how, one evening at the beginning of January, she found herself sitting opposite him at his little table in the attic. Both felt equally nervous, Peter's shy manner making Anne feel very gentle and also eager to know what was going on inside him. At the same time, she wished he would look beyond her ridiculous chatter to her real, much quieter, self. The evening passed and nothing happened.

Later Anne felt that the whole situation was far from encouraging. The idea that she should beg for Peter's attention was simply distasteful. There was no question of her being in love. If the Van Pelses had had a daughter instead of a son, Anne would have tried to make friends with her instead. That night she had a dream about another Peter, Peter Wessel, whom she had adored when she was a small child. She did not foresee that Peter Wessel and Peter Van Pels would eventually grow into one person, for whom she longed desperately.

It was nearly February. The rows and arguments in the Annexe had not slackened. On her birthday, Mrs Frank privately expressed the wish not to see the Van Pelses for a fortnight. Anne, reflecting upon the problems of cohabitation, decided that it was fine to have learned a bit about human nature, but now she thought she had learned enough. Meanwhile, she tried to make Margot's eighteenth birthday on 16 February as nice as possible for her sister.

March came at last, signalling the end of the cold, dark days. It was clear that Germany would lose the war. Nevertheless, the invasion was long in coming. The inhabitants of Amsterdam were ill and undernourished;

A letter to Kitty from Anne's diary
Copyright ANNE FRANK – Fonds, Basel

The kitchen in the Secret Annexe

everyone was wearing old clothes and old shoes. From the beginning of 1944, the Nazis shot many Dutch resistance fighters. In March, the people who supplied the group with illegal food-ration coupons were caught by the Gestapo. The atmosphere in the secret den became more dreary and dejected, as did the food, which now consisted mainly of porridge, potatoes and a kind of hash made from kale.

On Sunday, April 9, burglars broke into the warehouse. When Miep and Jan Gies came to the offices in the morning, they discovered a huge hole in the front door and the whole place turned upside down. Miep hurried upstairs to the bookcase. She whistled to the people inside to unlatch it. Then she swung the door open and rushed on up to the second floor with her husband

close at her heels. Never had she seen the
Secret Annexe in such disorder: the table had
not been cleared, and there was a jumble of
magazines, two half-eaten loaves of bread, a
mirror, a comb, and countless other items
piled on top of it. At the sight of Miep, Anne
ran and threw her arms around her neck. She
was in tears. The others gathered round for
reassurance. They were all trembling. The
night before, they had heard a noise and had
gone down into the warehouse to investi-
gate. Discovering that there were intruders
in the building, they had crept back upstairs,
terrified, to the Van Pels' room. Then they
had tried to keep still all night until their
helpers arrived. Luckily nothing terrible had
happened, but the burglary had reminded
everyone of the ever-present danger they
were in.

Meanwhile, Anne and Peter had drawn closer together. For a time, Peter had been shy and avoided Anne, making her feel miserable and lonely. But, after a while, she had learned to talk to him and they had become more at ease with one another. Peter started talking to her about his past, about his parents and about himself. Anne wondered if he was going to fall in love with her after all. Yet, how and when they were going to reach each other, she did not know.

By this stage, the adults had become very curious about what Anne and Peter were discussing together in the attic. Mrs Frank gave queer looks and made disapproving comments about her daughter's trips. Mrs Van Pels was jealous that her son no longer confided in her.

15 April, 1944, was an important day in Anne's life, the day of her first kiss. She recorded the moment in her diary. At eight o'clock in the evening, Anne was sitting with Peter on his divan. It was not the first time they had sat like that, but they had never sat so closely together. When the time came to part at half-past eight, Peter put on his gym-shoes while Anne stood beside him. How it happened so suddenly she did not know, but before they went downstairs he kissed her through her hair, half on her left cheek, half on her ear. Anne tore downstairs without looking around, and simply longed for the next day.

Love wasn't the only thing on Anne's mind in that spring of 1944. In the Secret Annexe the conversation was always about the impending Allied landing. There were many arguments about when the invasion would be. The helpers hoped it would come soon. With all the food shortages, they were not sure how much longer they could keep feeding the eight people in their care. Then, on 6 June, news of the Normandy invasion caused a stir among the inmates of the Annexe. They listened to General Eisenhower's announcement, wiping the tears from their eyes. It assured them that total victory would come within a year.

Six days after the Normandy invasion, it was Anne's fifteenth birthday. Peter had blushingly asked Miep to find some pretty flowers for Anne – a bunch of lavender peonies – which he duly presented to her. Besides the lovely bunch from her admirer, Anne also received several books, a handkerchief, a double bracelet from Margot, sweet peas from Mr Pfeffer, and sweets and exercise books from Miep and Bep. She felt thoroughly spoiled.

The exercise books were a lifeline for Anne. Without them she had no paper for her diary-keeping and scribbling. As her diary proves, she was a born writer with a talent for drawing character and describing scenes vividly. By her fifteenth birthday, she had discovered that her greatest wish, apart from getting married and having children, was to become a journalist or famous writer. Besides her diary, she was writing other things: fables, reminiscences, short stories and essays, some of which she read to her companions. One of the subjects she had in mind for a book was an account of their life in the Secret Annexe.

Dit is een foto, zoals
ik me zou wensen,
altijd zo te zijn.
Dan had ik nog wel
een kans om naar
Holywood te komen

Anne Frank.
10 Oct. 1942

"This is a (translation)
a photo as I would wish
myself to be all the time.
I would maybe have a chance to
come to Hollywood."
Anne Frank, 10 Oct. 1942

A photograph and a wish from Anne's diary

German troops surrender to the Allies in Belgium

THE ARREST

The end of July 1944 saw the beginning of
the great Allied offensive which was to lead
to the liberation of France and Belgium
within a month. There was a feeling of
hope in the Secret Annexe, especially when
they heard on Friday, 21 July, that an attempt
had been made on Hitler's life. By now,
more than two years had passed since they
had gone 'underground'.

At about half-past ten on the morning of 4

August 1944, a pleasant summer's day, a car drew up outside the offices on the Prinsengracht. A man in the uniform of the Austrian police, accompanied by Dutch policemen and several others in civilian clothes got out of the car and ran into the building, where Miep, Bep, Mr Kleiman and Mr Kugler were sitting at work. With a sinking heart, Miep realised that they had had it. The five policemen knew everything. They ordered Mr Kugler to take them upstairs to the bookcase. Then, drawing their revolvers, they went inside. It is not known who betrayed the hiding place to the Germans.

While the people upstairs were being arrested, Bep was able to walk out of the building. Miep stayed behind with Mr Kleiman and Mr Kugler. Though she escaped arrest, they were taken with the others in a truck to a Dutch police station. (Later Mr Kleiman and Mr Kugler were interned in a camp, which they both survived.) By now, it was about one o'clock. Miep found and took care of Peter's cat, Mouschi, who had run away during the commotion.

At the end of that afternoon, Miep, Bep, and Van Maaren, the warehouseman, slipped back upstairs to the Secret Annexe. It was in chaos. The pages of Anne's diary, as well as other papers and the family's photo album, lay scattered on the floor. Miep gathered them up and put them in her desk. About a week later, the Secret Annexe was emptied on German orders.

Meanwhile, on 8 August, the eight people from the Secret Annexe were transferred to the Westerbork concentration camp in the north of Holland. A survivor from Westerbork recalled that when the party arrived their faces were as white as paper from living in hiding for so long. They stayed in Westerbork for the whole of the month of August, and Anne and Peter were often together. Surprisingly, Anne looked radiant and her beauty seemed to flow into Peter. Hardly a word was spoken by Edith Frank and Margot, who both seemed numbed by the new situation. Mr Frank was quiet too, but it was a reassuring quietness that helped Anne and the other people in the camp. Though he lived in the men's barracks, he came and visited Anne every evening when she fell ill, standing by her bed for hours and telling her stories.

At the beginning of September, the group from the Secret Annexe were sent in cattle-trucks to Auschwitz, the extermination centre in German-occupied Poland. By this time, eighty-five trains had left Westerbork for the two death camps in Poland, Sobibor and Auschwitz, and one for Theresienstadt; and more than a million people, the majority of them Jews, had been gassed at Auschwitz. The first thing Anne and her family saw of Auschwitz, when they arrived on the night of 5 September, were the glaring searchlights fixed on the train. Once they were on the platform, the men and women were separated. While Mr Frank, Mr Pfeffer, Mr Van Pels and Peter went one way, Anne, her sister, her mother and Mrs Van Pels had to make the hour's march to the women's barracks at Auschwitz-Birkenau. The very next day, 549 people from this last train were sent to the gas chambers.

Under the terrible conditions of life in Auschwitz, the older members of the party weakened. Mr Van Pels was selected for the gas chamber and put to death just a few weeks after arriving. Mr Frank escaped this fate by a strange twist of fortune which brought him to the camp hospital in November. Meanwhile, his wife and two daughters were losing their strength. Though Anne was still lively and sweet, her gaiety had vanished. And yet, she showed great qualities of courage and endurance. A survivor of Auschwitz recalled how Anne distributed the bread in the barracks so well and so fairly that there was none of the usual grumbling.

At the end of October, Mrs Frank and her two girls, together with other prisoners, had to report for a selection. It meant filing into

Graves of prisoners who died after the liberation
of Bergen-Belsen

Otto Frank transcribed Anne's diaries after the war
Copyright ANNE FRANK – Fonds, Basel

the barracks where a doctor stood by a searchlight for the examination. Mrs Frank went first and was picked for the group of the old and sick. Then it was the turn of the two girls. Anne encouraged Margot, who walked into the searchlight. There they stood for a moment and then walked on. It was the last Mrs Frank saw of her daughters. Margot and Anne had to leave their mother behind at Auschwitz, as they and Mrs Van Pels had been selected to go to another camp at Bergen-Belsen in Germany. Alone in Auschwitz, Mrs Frank survived for another two months. She died on 6 January 1945, broken by the horrors she had experienced.

When the Frank sisters arrived at Bergen-Belsen, conditions, as in all the camps, were indescribable. Prisoners were crammed to-

gether in unheated barracks where conta-
gious diseases raged. Tens of thousands of
people died in the last months of the war
alone. It was winter. Like everyone else,
Anne and Margot did not have enough
food or water or warm clothes. They were
made to sleep in a tent, which was soon
destroyed by a storm. After several months
they both caught typhus. One day in late
February or early March, Margot died. Her
sister's death broke Anne's spirit. She gave
way to her own illness and died a few days
later. She was fifteen. It was just a few weeks
before British soldiers liberated Bergen-Belsen.

Mr Frank was the only one of the group to
survive the camps. He was still in Auschwitz
when the Russian army liberated the camp
on 27 January 1945. With a few other

survivors he was moved across Galicia to the Black Sea port of Odessa, where a New Zealand ship picked them up and brought them back to western Europe. The other prisoners in the camp had been evacuated by the Germans as the Russians advanced. Among them were Fritz Pfeffer, who died in the Neuengamme concentration camp on 20 December 1944, and Peter Van Pels, who died in Mauthausen on 5 May 1945. The last person from the Secret Annexe, Mrs Van Pels, died after leaving the Theresienstadt camp in the spring of 1945.

THE DIARY

After the war, Mr Frank returned to Amsterdam on 3 June 1945. He went straight from the station to see Miep and Jan Gies. By then he knew that his wife, Edith, would not be coming back, but he still had hopes of seeing Margot and Anne again. Miep immediately made him welcome and told him that he could stay with them for as long as he liked.

Resuming work as the head of his old firm in the offices on Prinsengracht, Mr Frank

Jan and Miep Gies in later years with a model of the house

Otto Frank receives an award for the sale of
1 million copies of the Diary

searched daily for news about his daughters. Two months passed. One morning at the beginning of August, as he and Miep were opening the office mail, a letter arrived, telling him of the fate of Margot and Anne. Miep saw Mr Frank walk towards his private office, and heard the door close. Overcome with emotion herself, she sat down at her desk.

All this time, Miep had kept Anne's writings locked in the drawer of her desk. She took the papers to Mr Frank in his office and pressed them into his hands. Then she left him to read Anne's work in peace.

Moved and astonished by what he read, Mr Frank decided to make a copy of the diary on a typewriter, at the same time translating large parts of it into German so that his mother could read it. Later he gave copies of the transcript to friends and acquaintances, who urged him to publish it.

At first it was difficult to find a publisher. However, one of the people who read the manuscript was a well-known Dutch historian, Professor Jan Romein. He was so impressed that he wrote an enthusiastic article about it, published on 3 April 1946 in the Dutch newspaper *Het Parool*. He said that although some two hundred similar diaries had been written during the war, it would be hard to find another one 'as lucid, as intelligent and, at the same time, as natural'.

The article caused a stir. A publisher was found. The diary came out in Dutch in the summer of 1947, under the title *Het Achter-*

huis (The Secret Annexe). The unanimously favourable reviews praised the intelligence, honesty and insight with which Anne had observed herself and her surroundings, and described the diary as one of the most poignant books in Occupation literature. By 1950, the Dutch edition was already in its sixth impression.

In 1952, *The Diary of a Young Girl* by Anne Frank appeared in England as well as the United States. Since then it has been translated into at least fifty-five different languages, and more than 24 million copies of the book have been sold in over fifty-five countries.

Mr Frank had now fulfilled Anne's wish to become a writer. In 1952, he moved from Amsterdam to Switzerland. In 1953, he retired from his position as director of the company at Prinsengracht. That same year, he married Elfriede Geiringer-Markovits, who was also a survivor of Auschwitz. They settled in Basel, where Mr Frank died in August 1980, at the age of ninety-one. He donated the pages of Anne's diary to the State of the Netherlands. The house at Prinsengracht 263, where the Frank family lived in hiding for two years and thirty days, was opened to the public as a museum in 1960. Every year it is visited by about 600,000 people from all over the world.

CHRONOLOGY

1889

Otto Frank is born in Frankfurt on 12 May.

1925

Otto marries Edith Hollander in Aachen on 12 May.

1926

Otto and Edith's first daughter Margot is born.

1927

the family moves to the house on Marbach-weg.

1929

Anne Frank is born in Frankfurt on 12 June.

1931

The family moves to Ganghoferstrasse.

1933

Adolf Hitler becomes Chancellor of Germany in January. The Jewish mayor of Frankfurt is forced to resign and all Jewish public employees are dismissed from their posts. Otto and Edith Frank resolve to leave Germany.

In the summer Edith and the children stay at her mother's house in Aachen while Otto goes to look for work and for a place for the family to live in Amsterdam.

In September, Otto registers his new business, the Opekta-Works, with the Amsterdam Chamber of Industry and Commerce.

1934

Edith, Margot and Anne join Otto in Amsterdam, followed by Edith's mother. They share a flat on the Merwedeplein in South Amsterdam.

Anne and Margot join the nearby Montessori school and learn Dutch.

Some 24,000 Jewish refugees have by now arrived in Holland from Germany.

1939

War breaks out in Europe.

1940

German troops occupy Holland after the invasion on 10 May. The Nazi persecution of Dutch Jews begins, with increasing restrictions on public life and with the 'dejudification' of Dutch businesses.

Otto Frank transfers the ownership of his business to Mr Kugler and Mr Kleiman.

1941

Anne and Margot are forced to leave the Montessori school following the racial segregation of schools.

1942

All Jews are forced to wear the yellow star.

Otto Frank tries to arrange for his family to emigrate, and begins preparations for a secret hiding place behind the offices at Prinsengracht 263.

In July, Margot receives orders to report at a 'labour' camp. The family decide to go into hiding immediately. Miep and Jan Gies help to install them in the Secret Annexe. The Franks are joined by the Van Pels family.

Nazis round up increasing numbers of Jewish people for the concentration camps.

Anne begins to write her diary.

Fritz Pfeffer joins the families in the Annexe in November.

1943

The Allied bombing of German cities begins.

The families face new scares when the ownership of the building changes and again when the warehouse is burgled in July.

Italy surrenders to the Allies on 8 September.

1944

Anne falls in love with Peter. She has her fifteenth birthday on 12 June.

The secret Annexe is discovered by the police on 4 August. The families are sent to Westerbork concentration camp. The group is moved to Auschwitz on 5 September, and then separated.

Mr Van Pels dies in Auschwitz. Otto

Auschwitz prisoners after liberation

Frank is sent to the camp hospital. In October, Edith, Anne and Margot are moved with Mrs Van Pels to Bergen-Belsen. Fritz Pfeffer dies in the Neuengamme camp on 20 December.

1945

Edith Frank dies in Auschwitz on 6 January. Anne and Margot die of typhoid in the spring. Peter Van Pels dies in Mauthausen on 5 May. His mother dies in the spring after leaving the Theresienstadt camp.

Otto Frank, the only survivor, returns to Amsterdam. He finds Anne's diaries and transcribes them. They are first published in 1947.

LIFE AND TIMES

Julius Caesar
Hitler
Monet
Van Gogh
Beethoven
Mozart
Mother Teresa
Florence Nightingale
Anne Frank
Napoleon

LIFE AND TIMES

JFK
Martin Luther King
Marco Polo
Christopher Columbus
Stalin
William Shakespeare
Oscar Wilde
Castro
Gandhi
Einstein

FURTHER MINI SERIES
INCLUDE

ILLUSTRATED POETS

Robert Burns
Shakespeare
Oscar Wilde
Emily Dickinson
Christina Rossetti
Shakespeare's Love Sonnets

FURTHER MINI SERIES
INCLUDE

HEROES OF THE WILD WEST

General Custer
Butch Cassidy and the Sundance Kid
Billy the Kid
Annie Oakley
Buffalo Bill
Geronimo
Wyatt Earp
Doc Holliday
Sitting Bull
Jesse James

FURTHER MINI SERIES
INCLUDE

THEY DIED TOO YOUNG

Elvis
James Dean
Buddy Holly
Jimi Hendrix
Sid Vicious
Marc Bolan
Ayrton Senna
Marilyn Monroe
Jim Morrison

THEY DIED TOO YOUNG

Malcolm X
Kurt Cobain
River Phoenix
John Lennon
Glenn Miller
Isadora Duncan
Rudolph Valentino
Freddie Mercury
Bob Marley